Failed Poems Of A Failed Unknown.

Michael Sherbrooke

Copyright © Michael Sherbrooke
All Rights Reserved.

This book has been self-published with all reasonable efforts taken to make the material error-free by the author. No part of this book shall be used, reproduced in any manner whatsoever without written permission from the author, except in the case of brief quotations embodied in critical articles and reviews.

The Author of this book is solely responsible and liable for its content including but not limited to the views, representations, descriptions, statements, information, opinions, and references ["Content"]. The Content of this book shall not constitute or be construed or deemed to reflect the opinion or expression of the Publisher or Editor. Neither the Publisher nor Editor endorse or approve the Content of this book or guarantee the reliability, accuracy, or completeness of the Content published herein and do not make any representations or warranties of any kind, express or implied, including but not limited to the implied warranties of merchantability, fitness for a particular purpose.

The Publisher and Editor shall not be liable whatsoever...

Made with ❤ on the BookLeaf Publishing Platform
www.bookleafpub.in
www.bookleafpub.com

Dedication

I dedicate this book to the ideas of becoming, learning, imagining, and grace. To the children of tomorrow who will struggle as the children of yesterday have, but in their own way. I dedicate these poems to you, the reader.

But most importantly, I dedicate these poems to that lonely child I once was who dreamed of one day publishing a book of poems. Life didn't get much better, but, I'm still doing the things you once dreamed of doing despite that fact.

Preface

This book is a foray into an under-practiced but favored art of mine. I learned how to communicate and express myself through music and poetry when I was a kid. I loved peering into the worlds and minds of others as a way to compensate for never having any social groups that I belonged to or anyone who was a trustworthy or reliable friend until the 8th grade.

I've been through poverty, parental abandonment, excessively traumatic bullying, told by even teachers and a principle that I either deserved what was happening to me or that I didn't belong in their schools because of the things that made me different, and more. I've seen too much with my eyes and heard too much with my ears and now I think far too much with my mind and feel too much with my heart.

You should expect these themes and others to come up in the works collected in this book.

Acknowledgements

I would like to thank a few people who've touched my life in one way or another.

First, there was Mrs. Donnay who I'm not sure that I'm spelling her last name correctly. She was my Catholic Elementary school teacher in Fergus Falls, Minnesota and the impact she had on my life as a child who wasn't like his classmates could never be understated.

I thank my mom for doing her best to raise my brother and I despite all of the many struggles she went through as a single mother dealing both with undiagnosed ADHD and Autism Spectrum Disorder. Especially after my Dad abandoned all of us for several years and stopped picking my brother and I up for his weekends. I learned so much from her resilience and overcoming strength. I appreciate she had no other "right" choice, but even still, there were countless wrong ones she would never have been blamed for that she refused to make.

I'd also like to thank John, who came to sit with me one random day in the 8th grade and was the first person in my life to honestly want to be my friend. I can't say for sure or not, and we haven't spoken in years, but, I think you might have saved my life, John. Thank you.

I want to thank my brother who, even though we rarely got along well as kids, he's always had my back when I never realized it. He may be my younger brother, but, he's also more successful than me. I've learned a lot by being his brother. Despite being older, he was always more of a big brother to me than I feel like I was to him.

My grandma Reitan was also a huge positive influence on my life. I remember engaging sometimes in deeper conversations about people, religion, and the realities of the world. I will never forget how warm and accepting she was for me when I came out as gay during my teenage years. I was so scared because I thought her religion, and also being from a completely different generation than mine, would have seen her disown me. Especially after how my aunt and dad acted about it, that is to say unsupportively however and not harshly as to each of them. Like my mom, I sometimes wish she was still here, too.

I'd obviously also like to thank both my current dog, Mason, and my late dog, Marley, for making me smile and laugh when I felt hollow. Laying with me on cold nights as we kept each other warm. And giving me, if nothing else, a logical reason to not listen to the demands of my worst depressions. They both have made my life so much richer just for having existed within it and that's worth more than any lottery ever could be to me.

I'd also like to thank everyone I work with at my current job. Not just my immediate coworkers, the kitchen crew, but those in the other departments of the retirement and care facility we all work at. Even the residents who live there. I've been directly exposed to so many stories, so many lifetimes, so many personal histories at that job and I value absolutely all of it. I cherish my coworkers who let me be myself around them no matter how weird, depressing, political, hyper, overstimulated, or otherwise obnoxious I could get at times. Thank you for being not just my coworkers, but also for being my friends.

Sometimes, I cry just thinking how grateful I am to all of you. I'm so bad at telling any of you any of that, though, so I wanted to make sure to say it all here. Thank you. All of you.

1. We Spoke

I died and died and died again,
The people danced as merry men,
The children played with each their friends,
But I... — I failed to ever be like them...

We spoke, of course... —
We spoke with words, though.
The kind that talking hurts like whores.
We spoke, but only through revolving doors.

I looked into your eyes and saw,
The hints of countless battles fought,
The judgements that I think you thought,
So many things of which we never talked.

I wonder, though, my fellow soul,
Did you peer into my own?
Seen the things I hate I know?
The words I trap within my throat?

Yes, we spoke, we kept it sweet.
Like a freshly honeyed tea.
But I was dead behind my speech,
And all the dead in me, —

— Saw the dead in you as I listened to you speak.

2. Lie beside my darling

Darling,
The liar made his lies your truths,
Now my blood drips from your hands.
Taste it darling, and swallow truth.
This blood of mine, is now your proof.

Darling,
The liar told you true was false.
Now our house belongs to him.
I do not blame you, darling, no.
But now my blood is on our walls.

Darling,
I forgive you, — it's true. I do.
I do not blame you or our guns
Not your rage, and not the noose.
But darling, a lie, — is still a lie.

Now my body lies like death beside you.

3. Broken News

The news is spewing hate again —
"Blame the other."
"Blame each other."
I wish that I was deaf...
But then I'd never hear a bird again,
A laugh again,
A song again,
Or even when the news is good.

The news is showing pain again —
"Starving children."
"Alarming violence."
I wish that I was blind...
But then I'd never see the sky again,
A smile again,
A flower again,
Or even when the news is good.

The news is not the news again —
Partisan talk,

Partisan plot,
I wish I couldn't think...
But then I'd never dream again,
Write again,
Understand again,
Or even know when the news is finally good.

4. Cynical Optimism

Did hear me say I'm fine?
It's a lie of course, please don't mind,
Because it's nearly time.
"For what?"
For human destiny to climb the vine.

Did you hear the news?
The partisan said it's time to choose.
They said it's me vs you.
"They did?"
Yes, they did, but we know it isn't true.

Did you feel things shift today?
I think we're gonna be okay.
The human spirit is in play.
"Could you explain?"
The people are finally more awake.

It hurts my heart to see the blaze
But I know this is the only way...

The old moralities have rotted all away,
    And the new moralities, —

    — They're here to stay.

5. Always Never

I am nothing, I never was.
"Don't say that."
"You should know that you are loved."
Is love the hand of poverty,
Leaving children hungry?
I do not need a love like that.

I am no one, I never was.
"No, don't say that."
"You are loved and you are strong."
Is strength the life of tragedy,
Which robs us of our dignity?
I do not need a strength like that.

I am lost, I always was.
"Why say that?"
"You are strong and you are wise."
Is wisdom the act of breaking,
Upon every morning's waking?
I don't need wisdom that's as that.

I am gone, I always was.
"How is that?"
"You are wise, and you are home."
Is home the place that traps you there,
Forcing out your lung's own air?
I do not need that kind of home.

This life of mine, you try to soothe —
Has stripped of me my future's hue...
"But you are loved!"
"You are strong!"
"You are wise and you are —"
— Nothing.

I always never was...

6. The Witness Prayer

Did you hear my prayer tonight?
I prayed for they who brave the fight.
The ones from lands beyond my sight,
For this world as mine is too their right.

I'm sending out a prayer tonight.

Did you hear my prayer for them?
I prayed in hope they'd circumvent,
The whims of despot partisans.
To have a people's government.

I'm sending out a prayer for them.

Did you hear their prayers, oh God?
Free them from all liars' frauds.
Remove from us each source of rot.
For we all share this earthly plot.

They're sending out their prayers, oh God.

Did you see them fight for it?
The peace they feared could be forfeit.
The dreams they held in deep remit.
With justice dripping from their fists.

I pray you see them fight for it.

I spent my life in prayer for this.
The old ways to vanish into mist,
As resistance sparks with human grit,
To feel the world become resistance.

I spent my life in prayer for this, —
Now I'll be my prayer's own witness.

7. Hope Insane

Since the day they mocked me gay,
I've often wandered through malaise,
Lost and gray,
I ran away,
But most importantly,
I hoped alone in vain.

I walked their road of broken thrones,
And wandered through their graves, deposed.
Kings dethroned,
Plans furloughed,
But most importantly,
I found a stain of hope.

They tortured even holy men,
Made them bleed and made them bend,
Refused amends,
Then shot their heads.
But most importantly,
They hurt our friends.

Since the part where broke my heart,
I've often wondered how to start,
To make my art,
Or just embark,
But most importantly,
Not lose my spark.

Since the day they mocked me gay,
Made a child sorrows slave.
I'm not brave.
I'm not a bane.
This is what's important, please,—
I will always hope alone in vain...

Because, my friend,
My hope's insane.

8. Flowers for Abigail

I never knew a girl named Abigail,
Was she sweet and beautiful?
Did she dance through storms of hail?
Was her smile wide and full?

I never knew a girl named Abigail, —
But I brought her flowers both blue and pale.

I heard she had a favorite song,
Was it one she sung with Mom?
Or maybe she just hummed along?
I wonder if it kept her strong?

I never knew a girl named Abigail, —
But I brought her flowers, both red and blonde.

Did she dream of future's far?
Like raising horses on the farm?
Or finding one to give her heart?
Perhaps the first to walk on Mars?

I never knew a girl named Abigail, —
But I brought her flowers both light and dark.

I never did and never will,
Get chance to know Miss Abby Trill.
Thirteen injured and seven killed,
At that school, atop that hill.

I never knew a girl named Abigail, —
But I brought her flowers that can not wilt...

I never knew a girl named Abigail, —
And now I never will...

9. A home I've never known

I want to go home to a place I've never known.
A place where children never die,
Get hit, or left alone, —
With thoughts that only echo.

A place that feels like home.

Where nature grows and creatures roam,
And people thrive to tend their grove.
A place of which no king's hold thrones,
And dragons hoard neither gold nor bones.

I want to go home to a place I've never known.
A place where people have a soul,
And hearts that grow, —
So they may have an endless hope.

I want to go somewhere I've never known,
A place that finally feels like home.

10. Silence

When breath is heavy as body's drop,
And tired eyes may water crops,
A child screams in silence; —
Muted by the tones of loss.

I felt the claw across my breast,
Of a peace the likes of death,
I wept alone in silence; —
Cradled by a life of much bereft.

I close my eyes to dream of awe,
The likes of which I never saw,
A home becomes of silence; —
To grant me all I truly want.

I felt it nudge me gentle like,
Told me that it didn't mind,
I lived my life so silent; —
That I never made that much of life.

It told me that it couldn't judge,
That it could take away my every grudge,
And deliver me from silence; —
It only asked of me my trust.

Now you know my closest friend,
The one who saw me hurt and mend,
You'll find it hard, his name pronounced; —
Because he leaves if you aren't silent.

His name, my friend, is simply...

Silence.

11. Small

Dear friend,

Have you heard the death toll lately?
They say it's greater than a tragedy.
I even heard they named an enemy.
But, I cannot understand, —
They said that it was me...

Speaking of, I saw a pretty flower today.
It was tall and yellow and made me want to pray.
Then the butterflies stole my mind away.
You should have seen them, —
They glowed like sunlit golden rays...

The cold season is starting soon...
The trees are turning vibrant hues.
So much beauty despite the news.
The taste of this is bitter, —
Like how peels taste comparative to juice...

Have you ever paused to watch at all,
The life of something that's both weak and small?
Observing as it climbs and crawls,
Despite its limits and its faults?

That is to say I'm scared, dear friend, —
That I'm not safe within these walls...

12. Not-so-different

Once upon a not-so-different time, —
A not-so-different place or life,
I was a boy of Catholic tribe.
I lived right on that dreaded line, —
You call it poverty, they called it fine,
Either way, my mother tried, —

... so hard she tried.

In a rather not-so-different land, —
To raise two sons by single hand,
And raise them each a proper man.
Relying on such payment plans, —
As those of an assistance program,
Or money from a divorced dad.

That was all we really had.

When came a not-so-different year, —
In which my father disappeared,

As if he didn't want me near... —
Years had passed, no voice to hear,
Until he met a strong-willed country dear,
Who found him nursing on a beer.

He was unmoved by his own son's tears...

I remember in a locker room, —
In a not-so-different school,
At hands of those both mean and cruel;
My childhood would end undue.
The adults said it wasn't true, —
What other students forced me through.

Some adults had blamed me, too...

As young as ten I chased for death, —
Attempted twice to draw no breath,
Then was on a psyche ward bed.
Months had past, but that was when, —
"You're going home," that's what they said.
But within a year, I was back again...

My classmates all but made me dead...

Now in this not-so-different day, —
These ghosts of mine are here to stay.

No one will make them go away.
You'll see them in my smile's shape, —
When you always hear me say,
"I promise I'm okay."

But don't most folks hurt, —
In such these not-so-different ways?

13. Breaking Free

I do not credit widened eyes,
To crickets chirping in my pain,
The drip - drip - drip of lifelong cries,
But I will not give that pain a shrine.

I see the flesh which wraps my bones,
How it bleeds but feels no shame,
The torture of a child's hone,
But I do not thank the pain alone.

I thank the beauty of the creek,
The fresh-land air upon the breeze,
The way they give my hurt some peace,
I shall not liken pain to these.

The forge is found in principle,
Not any school of crucible.
Suffering makes one cynical,
But it does not make them venerable.

Do not thank the treachery,
But thank yourself for breaking free.

14. The Crucible of Empathy

I know something born of empathy.
A path forsaken easily.
So readily.
As if to do so was a victory and not a tragedy.

I truly know you not,
You sordid fools of moral rot;
Who cling to faith so strained and fraught,
Instead of loving like your God.

There is no honor in what you say.
It's all decay.
It's all disdain.
You call it strength that you display.

But what you speak is savagery.
I've seen the beast.
Don't you see?
He dressed up as the family priest.

Have not you heard the children weep?
They weep with me.
Silently.
In this Crucible of Empathy.

I know something born of empathy.
A path forsaken easily.
So readily.
As if to do so would somehow set them free.

Though I am safe, I broke my mind.
With bleeding eyes,
I didn't look away,
From that horrid sanctioned genocide...

A headless future with no grave.
A spent grenade.
A baby's face.
I've seen the malice of your faith.

How can you question our morality?
It's hypocrisy.
It's moral laziness.
Look within then out before you speak.

Have not you heard the angels weep?
They walk with me,

On pilgrimage.
In this Crucible of Empathy.

I embrace my curse of empathy.
The destruction that it does to me.
So readily.
For I've seen its bloody moral majesty.

I've seen the vintage eyes,
Of those you've ostracized.
Terrified,
Of becoming people you politicize.

You are the salesmen of division.
Who with precision,
And with a mission.
Try to paint the innocent as demons.

How can you claim with certainty,
Maliciously,
Rapaciously,
That the righteous way is apathy?

Have not you heard the people weep?
They weep with me.
So vibrantly.
In this Crucible of Empathy.

My self-directed tyranny is empathy.
A path that makes my ego grieve,
And hate to breathe.
But I've seen its peaceful violent clarity .

The Crucible of Empathy,
Will cull what makes the people weak.
By granting you,
The strength it takes to seek,

The truth of human destiny.

15. Alchemy of Thought

Sometimes when I feel a thought,
Tugging at my mind in colors nearly any shade,
I feel it like a nudging hand to guide me to a pleasant spot.
To a thinker, it's almost like a hand grenade.

I watch it burst, and bang, and bloom,
But then I change the color's hue,
Watch it turn to something new,
I felt it as the red of rage but what about as sorrow's blue?

Have you ever thought to try it?
To think of something that amuses or astounds,
As if it may be something tragic?
I often think of what is simple, but feel it as profound.

I feel it breathe, I feel it teethe.
The torment of analysis addicts the fancy of my will.
It's as if the truth is not philosophy,

But instead the murmurs of the trees that defy the
seasons chill.

The more I come to learn myself,
The more eluded I become.
Deluded by the old ways knell,
I find my worries never quell yet they cease to drum and
drum.

An emotion lies within me,
I'm not it nor is it feeling I possess.
I give to it my thinking alchemy,
To watch it morph, and warp, and let me bear it witness.

Sometimes, when a thought is found,
Somewhere in my human mind,
I build for it a tiny town,
So in me a home it finds.

16. A Name

I never had a name worth finding.
Did I ever want one?
I feel it on this road winding.
I think I only wanted love.

It's strange at times, I think,
That we so easily take to drink,
From cups of hate, filled to brink.
Perhaps that's why we never win?

Look outside and see the trees.
Hear the birds and feel the breeze.
I never had a name worth finding,
Until I found it in the leaves.

The rich men there in Washington,
They'll never lead, they lack conviction.
People cry, they die, then go to work again.
While the wealthy practice nepotism.

You see it, too, I know you do.
They want us fighting, red vs. blue.
While they dismantle every due,
And every great thing built for me and you.

I never had a name worth finding,
Until I found it in our graves.
The light we seek is oh so blinding,
But in it's ways we'll forge and make, —

Ourselves some names worth finding.

17. Another Life

Maybe in another life,
Another dream, another time...
We aren't alone as thinking beasts,
Nor even as one's seeking light.

The children will each laugh and play,
With different ilk, of different ways.
I'll be a kid myself again,
In a home where all is right each day.

I wake up in a healthy place,
Greet my parents, —
Eat my breakfast, —
Leave for school before I'm late.

Maybe in this other life,
I won't go through it all alone.
I'll never think of suicide,
Like I have since all I've known.

I'll have some truly honest friends.
I'll live as how a child should,
With love and warmth instead of meds.
I'll live a life I'll truly want to never end.

Maybe in another life, —
I'll never witness violent blood,
I will not hate to hold a knife,
And finally know a life of love...

18. Trophies

In this gilded modern age,
I read a post of someone say,
"Don't look at these wounds,
They do not define me!"

An image of a wounded beast.
A broken heart,
And frightened mind.
An image of a lonely spark.

I paused in thought.
I had to stop.
I was inspired by what I'd saw.
So I had to write, how could I not?

Despite my rather cynic mind,
The aches I hide with smiles wide,
I boast as Trophies,
"Look what I survived!"

19. American Lie

Once I was a young, young boy.
They said the world was mine.
That the evils had all been destroyed,
And America was a nation sanctified.
What a lie, — a horrid, horrid lie.

I work to rent, — it never ends.
I give and give my time to spend.
Then the red hat's in the news again.
They're selling you your patriotism.
Oh, how they lie, — dividing you and I.

Once I was a young, young boy.
They said the world was mine.
I dreamed of traveling all the world,
See the vistas of an earth sublime.
Then I cried, — oh, how it was I cried.

I live to work, — I work to live.
Make no progress, then goodnight.

Then the red hat sells another lie.
Then turns you to a red hat Reich.
Getting rich off each lie you buy.

Once I was a young, young boy,
And I saw the people crying out for hope.
I saw the faithful playing coy.
America's not sanctified, it's hanging by a rope.
And that rope is made of lies... —

Such horrid, horrid lies; —
Corrosive, toxic lies; —
Greedy, treasonous lies; —
they sold to you and I. —
Such horrid, — sinful, sinful lies.

20. For the Record

Record profits, —
Record poverty, —
It's almost like the two are linked.
Hand in hand like joined twins.

Record protests, —
Record disparity, —
It's almost like they're both connected.
Like Jim Crow and the Wilmington reds.

Record violence, —
Record indignity, —
It's almost like one precedes the other.
As shelves of clouds bring with them thunder.

Record resistance, —
Record instability, —
We rise because we know we must.
To face the madmen of such petty lust.

21. The World I see

I wish that you could see,
the world it is, I see.
From star to shining sea,
The forest and its trees,
Each share our every history.

Each crown alike,
These towns, these lights
Each drowns and dies.
From sundown time to sunrise sight,
The spirits grow, these spirits plight.

We are, it seems, impermanence,
It's why we rage and menace,
Seek witnesses for our penance,
And struggle with intelligence.
But we're also pure resistance.

But in the world I see, you see,
We're less defined by treachery,

Than by resiliency and empathy.
All the nations that ended bloody,
Are the fertile soil of our destiny.

In the world, it is I see,
We grow from every tragedy,
We learn from every memory,
And dream of human destiny,
In the world I see... —

You and I are strong.
You and I are free.

www.ingramcontent.com/pod-product-compliance
Lightning Source LLC
Chambersburg PA
CBHW070501050426
42449CB00012B/3074